AUTHOR

Péter Mujzer served in the Hungarian Armed Forces for 20 years, graduated from the RCDS (Royal College of Defence Studies, London) and is now a military historian pursuing his PhD with a special interest in the Hungarian Armed Forces during the Second World War. He has already authored fifteen books and over fifty articles on related topics, many of them in English.

PUBLISHING'S NOTES

None of unpublished images or text of our book may be reproduced in any format without the expressed written permission of Luca Cristini Editore (already Soldiershop.com) when not indicate as marked with license creative commons 3.0 or 4.0. Luca Cristini Editore has made every reasonable effort to locate, contact and acknowledge rights holders and to correctly apply terms and conditions to Content.
Every effort has been made to trace the copyright of all the photographs. If there are unintentional omissions, please contact the publisher in writing at: info@soldiershop.com, who will correct all subsequent editions.
Our trademark: Luca Cristini Editore©, and the names of our series & brand: Soldiershop, Witness to war, Museum book, Bookmoon, Soldiers&Weapons, Battlefield, War in colour, Historical Biographies, Darwin's view, Fabula, Altrastoria, Italia Storica Ebook, Witness To History, Soldiers, Weapons & Uniforms, Storia etc. are herein © by Luca Cristini Editore.

LICENSES COMMONS

This book may utilize part of material marked with license creative commons 3.0 or 4.0 (CC BY 4.0), (CC BY-ND 4.0), (CC BY-SA 4.0) or (CC0 1.0). We give appropriate attribution credit and indicate if change were made in the acknowledgments field. Our WTW books series utilize only fonts licensed under the SIL Open Font License or other free use license.

For a complete list of Soldiershop titles please contact Luca Cristini Editore on our website: www.soldiershop.com or www.cristinieditore.com. E-mail: info@soldiershop.com

Title: **ITALIAN TANKS AND VEHICLES IN HUNGARIAN SERVICE** Code.: WTW-054 EN
By Péter Mujzer
ISBN code: 9791255890621 first edition January 2024
Language: English. Size: 177,8x254mm Cover & Art Design: Luca S. Cristini

WITNESS TO WAR (SOLDIERSHOP) is a trademark of Luca Cristini Editore, via Orio, 33/D - 24050 Zanica (BG) ITALY.

WITNESS TO WAR

ITALIAN TANKS AND VEHICLES IN HUNGARIAN SERVICE

HUNGARIAN-ITALIAN MILITARY COOPERATION AND ITALIAN MILITARY EQUIPMENT IN HUNGARIAN SERVICE DURING THE WW2

PHOTOS & IMAGES FROM WORLD WARTIME ARCHIVES

PÉTER MUJZER

BOOKS TO COLLECT

CONTENTS

Introduction .... pag. 5
   Hungarian army between wars .... pag. 5
   Hungarian-Italian military cooperation .... pag. 6
   Hungarian-Italian Armaments Committee .... pag. 11

Armoured vehicles .... pag. 15
   Fiat 3000 light tanks .... pag. 15
   CV33/35 - 35 M. FIAT Ansaldo *tankette* .... pag. 17
   Tankette units of the Hungarian Army .... pag. 27
   Operational history of the Ansaldo *tankettes* in Hungary .... pag. 31
   Further projects .... pag. 38

Italian vehicles in the Hungarian Army .... pag. 47
   Cars .... pag. 47
   Trucks .... pag. 55
   Motorcycles .... pag. 75

Artillery and infantry weapon's cooperation .... pag. 79

Uniforms and equipment .... pag. 89

Conclusions .... pag. 95

Bibliography .... pag. 97

INTRODUCTION

HUNGARIAN ARMY BETWEEN WARS

At the end of the First World War, Hungary, as a member of the k. und k. Monarchy, ended up on the losing side. Her army disintegrated and her armaments were either taken over or destroyed by the victorious Allied nations. In 1920 the Allied Powers gave the peace treaty of Trianon to Hungary, very similar to the one already imposed on Germany. The main military aspects of the peace treaty were as follows. Military service based on contracted soldiers, conscription was forbidden, and the army was to consist of no more than 35,000 men. Training of officers was restricted and the existence of a General Staff was prohibited. The formation of Gendarmerie, Police and Frontier Guard units was also curbed. All war materials, which could be found, were confiscated. The existence or use of aircrafts, guns larger than 105mm calibre, tanks and all heavy armaments was forbidden.

Hungarian diplomacy worked to form a close Italian, Austrian and Hungarian relationship in the late 1920s and early 1930s, to avoid isolation and to try to create a better position for Hungary among the European nations. In 1927 Hungary signed a treaty of co-operation with Italy. In the mid-1930s the international political situation changed. Germany had invalidated the Treaty of Versailles and begun to build up a modern regular army. To the Hungarians, Germany seemed to present the opportunity for a good alliance, perhaps providing the only support that Hungary could expect in its quest to recoup her losses of WWI.

The Hungarian Army, due to the limitations imposed by the Trianon Treaty, had a very limited capacity to protect the country. The available manpower was just enough to maintain internal security. The basic formation of the Army became the mixed brigade, four cavalry/hussar regiments and a few support units were also formed. The mixed brigades were composed of two infantry regiments, one artillery and one cyclist battalion, mortar and cavalry companies plus support units. Seven brigades were organised and were allocated to seven military districts within Hungary.

During the secret rearmament, the Hungarian Army initially concentrated on enlarging the personnel strength and in building up a supply of the equipment forbidden by the Treaty of Trianon. Starting in the mid-thirties, Hungary had a chance to purchase weapons and armaments from Italy and Germany and from neutral countries such as Sweden and Switzerland. The home-based military industry was also enlarged in accordance with the overall economic situation.

By 1938 the Hungarian Army had seven mixed brigades, one cavalry division, (two hussar brigades,) an aviation brigade, an experimental motorised group and the river forces. Under the direct command of the Chief of the General Staff were two heavy artillery battalions, four A/A artillery battalions, one signal battalion, one chemical warfare battalion, a mechanised transport regiment and an armoured group.

Following the announcement of armament equality with neighbouring countries in 1938, the enlargement of the Army began. Mixed brigades were reorganised into corps. Mobil troops were established, and the development of motorisation, air force and air defences began.

HUNGARIAN-ITALIAN MILITARY COOPERATION

Even though, during the Great War, the Hungarians and Italians were each other's unswerving enemies, finding themselves on opposing sides, the situation quickly eased after the war. The key figure who changed the hostile attitude of public opinion was Lieutenant Colonel Guido Romanelli, who was put in charge of the Italian Military Mission in Hungary from May 1919.

Romanelli worked to save many people from the terror of the Hungarian Bolsheviks. As early as June 1920, the Italian military mission agreed to supply surplus weapons to Hungary. This was mainly the material that had been recovered from the former armaments of the Austro-Hungarian monarchy, later recaptured as war booty by Italy. Material destined to quickly become obsolete, and the Italians were happy to sell it, at least in part. The shipment of such goods, formally forbidden by the Versailles agreements, was facilitated by the Polish-Soviet war.

It was agreed with the Polish government that the Polish army would be named as buyer and that the simultaneous Hungarian participation would be concealed on the documents of the war material shipments. Some goods trains on the Bologna-Warsaw rail route were therefore conveniently unloaded in Hungary and ammunition destined for the Poles was loaded in their place.

The Hungarian order, covered by the Polish deliveries, included 25,000 95-mm Manlicher rifles, 300 Schwarzlose machine guns, 40 100-mm 14 M. field howitzers, 12 18 M. 80-mm field guns, 12 15 M. 80-mm field guns, 8 75-mm mountain guns, 64 trucks, 8 motorbikes and 400 bicycles. However, there is no information on the exact amount of material delivered to Hungary.

On 5 April 1927, the Treaty of Friendship and Cooperation between Italy and Hungary was also signed in Rome, one of the most important tasks of which was to support the Hungarian armed forces. Hungarian Prime Minister István Bethlen raised with Benito Mussolini the necessity of rearming the Hungarian army and demanded the return and reparations of weapons seized by the Italians from the Habsburg Monarchy. Mussolini wanted the repairs to be carried out in Italy and specified a precise price for this, but formally did not ask for money for these arms supplies. The Hungarians also asked for other military loans and even aircraft from Italy.

Italy, trying to insert itself in the power vacuum created in Central Europe after the end of the Great War, also used the financial means to expand. The loans, and especially the military ones, had a special importance also because without them the rearmament of the Hungarian Army would not have been possible. Although military loans were the organic result of Italian economic policy aimed at encouraging the export of war materials. The late repayment was intended to avoid the insolvency of Italian military firms and resulted in the

▲ *Il Duce* talks to a Hungarian delegation during a military review, mid-1930s. State Archives.

purchase of Italian military equipment abroad, while the rather preferential interest rate paid by the Hungarian side even brought revenue to the Italian state. The first loan was followed by two others. However the first loan arrived Hungary only at the end of 1932. Due to the Great Economic Crisis and legal formalities. The first loan was followed by two others.

In the financial year 1930-1931 Italy supplied the Hungarian Army with 12 aircraft for 4.110.260 lire, 103 Pavesi artillery tractors and five FIAT B3000 light tanks for 10.889.740 lire. In the autumn of 1932 negotiations were also held on the purchase of artillery material. The Italians offered for sale mainly 150 mm and 21 mm heavy howitzers and 75 mm mountain guns.

On the other hand the Italians also interested in products designed and produced in Hungary. The Hungarian Government sold the licence of the Gebauer machine gun of Hungarian design to the Italians for 500.000, which was offset by the Italian Government's delivery of 32 decommissioned field guns. Italy sold the production rights to the "Pavesi" artillery tractor (P-4-100), cooperation was established on technical matters of aviation and, in the hope of an expected deal, the Italians also sent a CV33 *tankette*.

On 17 March 1934, the Rome Pact signed by Austria, Hungary and Italy, the three agreements focused on mutual political economic issues. In consequence of the Pact, over 490 machine guns and 42000 rifles were handed over to the Hungarian Army.

In 1935, to modernise its Air Force, the Hungarian government ordered 26 aircraft from the Italians. Among them 9 Ca-101 bombers were purchased for 695.000 lire each. The planes were brought to Szombathely by Italian pilots. In the same year, Italy started to deliver the unarmed CV33/35 *tankettes*.

For the fiscal year 1935/36, the Hungarian purchased 52 Cr.32 fighter aircraft and medium and heavy guns.

The final settlement of the $120 million freight transport loan for 1937-1938 consisted of:

- Artillery materials: 41.444.044 lire
- Engineer materials: 962.700 lire
- Clothing, equipment materials: 26.403.694 lire
- Medical materials: 331.546 lire
- Motor vehicles: 24.234.712 lire
- Chemical materials: 7.396.878 lire
- Aircrafts: 18.500.000 lire

Grand total: 119 273 576,70 lire

The largest amount was spent on artillery material; ammunition, bombs, primers, 75mm, 100mm, 150mm and 305mm shells and six 210mm 35 M heavy howitzers plus its equipment, while a fraction of the cost was spent on enlisted belts, rifle belts, ammunition pouches and holsters. For motor vehicles and other motorised material, 52 cars, 217 trucks, 19 off-road trucks, 16 tractors, a small number of workshop trucks, tankers and other special purpose military vehicles were received.

▲ Hungarian Colonel General Vilmos Rőder, Minister of Defence of Hungary, reviews a unit of Alpine troops during his visit to Italy in the late 1930s. (MTI)

Among the clothing and equipment materials, the settlement lists include tens of thousands of bedspreads, camp blankets, horse blankets, tents, as well as other textile items and leather.

Between 1939 and 1940, 300-300 million lire were drawn down from the loan facility. For this sum, Italy supplied mainly aircraft and motorvehicles, textile fabrics and leather, heavy artillery shells, projectiles and explosives, while at the same time substantial sums were paid to replace rapidly worn-out and obsolete Italian materials.

The most important procurements and programs aimed the modernisation of the Royal Hungarian Air Force:

- Pilots training in Italy for 200 men for 18.7413.00 lire
- Procurement of 70 Re.2000 fighter planes and its licence rights: 86.240.800 lire
- Procurement of 36 Ca.135 bomber planes: 73.574.323 lire
- Procurement of aviation ammunition and bombs: 94.675.245 lire

Grand total. 273 231 668 lire

One of the most important training courses was organised for the pilots of the Hungarian Air Force at South-Italy, Grottaglie. 200 young men, 100 officer and 100 NCO candidates; 50 reconnaissance, 60 fighter and 90 bomber pilots were trained in Italy, started in October 1938. The training was divided into three parts, basic, advanced and specialised training and ended in 1940.

The situation of Italian deliveries at the end of the 1940 financial year:

- Clothing and equipment: in this category, three-quarters of the more than 43 million lire was used to purchase blankets (bedspreads, horse blankets). More than 600 000 pieces were supplied by various Italian firms, a quantity that could cover the needs of a mobilised field army.
- Motor vehicles: 31.000.000 lire was spent on 86 Breda artillery tractors, 216 cars, a few dozen off-road vehicles, and special workshop and ambulance vehicles. More than half of the money was paid for artillery tractors.
- Artillery material: the Italian military industry undertook to supply 14 35 M 210mm howitzers and thousands of artillery shells and large quantities of gunpowder. The delivery was made in instalments and, after long delays, was not completed until the spring of 1942.
- Technical equipment. on this list the Italians also accounted for eight Galileo 120cm searchlights.
- Aviation material: these orders accounted for more than 80% of the Italian merchandise credit. The Italian aircraft factories supplied Hungary with 72 bombers, 138 fighters, 23 training aircraft, some 200 spare engines, large quantities of spare parts and bombs between 1938 and 1940.

Under the agreement of December 15, 1941, the arms loans were finally merged as "Prestito al Governo Ungherese", to be repaid at 4 percent interest over 15 years, with semi-annual repayments. The starting date was 1 April 1942 and the final date was 1 October 1956. The new combined loan amounted to 463 million lire.

HUNGARIAN-ITALIAN ARMAMENTS COMMITTEE

To coordinate concrete tasks of the military cooperation, a bilateral Armaments Committee was set up, headed by the Chief of the General Staff of both the Italian and Hungarian Armies. It was controlled by the head of the Military Technical Institute of the Hungarian and Italian Army, Lieutenant General Kornél Rumpelles and Lieutenant General Giuseppe Cortese. The Hungarian-Italian Armament Committee functioned from 1928 until 1944, the Committee held meetings yearly, two-three times in Rome or Budapest. The substantive work was carried out within the framework of the Armament Committee in the sub-committees (air defence, motorisation, communications, engineer, chemical warfare, arms, ammunition and explosives).

From 1934, new subcommittees (aircraft, artillery) were established.

The first exploratory talks on artillery weapons and ammunition began in 1928, when a Hungarian delegation visited the Italian Ansaldo factory to assess the extent to which the Italian partner could be involved (especially with regard to new cannons and ammunition) in the development of the Hungarian artillery. The members of the sub-commissions and delegations had reciprocal access to the Italian and Hungarian military and industrial facilities and visited the different military establishments: the Diósgyőr cannon and ammunition factory, the Fűzfő gunpowder factory, the Italian Arsenal in Piacenza, the Ansaldo cannon factory and the Odero-Terni arms factory.

From 1936 General Imre Bangha and General Alberto Gammera led the Committee.

Beside the military technology cooperation, visits, exchange programs, trainings were organised. Italian service manuals, handbooks of the new weapons (CV35 *tankettes*, heavy howitzers) were translated, adopted to Hungarian circumstances.

▲ Two Fiat 3000 tanks belonging to the Hungarian army, with the typical Hungarian three-colour camouflage and the Mechanised Branch insignia. They still lack the weapon as the Hungarians mounted Schwarzloses. (Bonhardt)

▲ Italian and foreign officers participate in a Hungarian field exercise in the late 1930s. The exchange of Italian and Hungarian officers was a common practice at the time. (MTI)

▼ Victor Emmanuel III, King of Italy visiting Hungary in the spring of 1937, seated next to Admiral Miklós Horthy, Governor of Hungary, in their car. (Fortepan)

▲ Italian officer surrounded by Hungarian ladies dressed in their traditional clothes during the celebration of the reconquest of the lost territories of Transylvania. (MTI)

▼ During the reconquest of Transylvania, Admiral Horthy greets Italian and German officers during the military parade in Nagyvárad (Oradea) on 7 September 1940. (Fortepan)

▲ The first Fiat 3000 light tanks that arrived in Hungary were painted olive-green with the Mechanised Branch insignia and without any weapons.

▼ The Fiat 3000s were later painted three colour, dirt yellow-dark brow-live green colours. The Hungarians mounted as their default weapon the Maschinengewehr Patent Schwarzlose M.07/12, well known to them as it was the service weapon of the Austro-Hungarian monarchy.

ARMOURED VEHICLES

Besides the aviation and artillery the Hungarians had high expectations to acquire modern armoured vehicles from Italy, which was not banned to develop and produce such weapons.

FIAT 3000 LIGHT TANKS

Secretly the Hungarians could purchase five FIAT 3000 light tanks, which were obsolete that time, but still acceptable for the Hungarians. The dismantled, unarmed vehicles arrived in Hajmáskér in March 1931 in the greatest secrecy.

The tanks were put into service with the help of Italian mechanics. The Hungarian military leadership was satisfied with the combat and technical performance of the FIAT 3000, and a possible licensed production of 150 units in Hungary was considered. The tanks were equipped with the Schwarzlose machine guns and were assigned to the Armoured Vehicle Battalion of the Police Recruit School (RUISK).

After that, the RUISK Tank Company had one FIAT 3000 and one LK-II tank platoon and one dummy armoured platoon built on a BMW car chassis. The FIAT tanks remained in service until 1938 and were later used as training vehicles. On 11 October 1940, the 1st Reconnaissance Battalion reported that its armoured training was carried out with two FIAT B3000 and a Polish Renault R-35 tank. In the early 1940s they were used as artillery targets.

▲ A FIAT 3000 light tank in service in Hungary in the mid-1930s; the soldier wears the Italian-style leather helmet, a distinctive piece of the uniform of armoured/motorcyclist troops. (Author collection)

▲ The FIAT 3000 light tanks received a two-digit number plate starting with H-. In the early 1940s, the light tanks were used for basic driving and mechanic training, at which point the turrets were removed. (Author collection) In the small photo, some Fiat 3000s and LK-II light tanks in the courtyard of a Hungarian barracks. (Bonhardt)

CV33/35 - 35 M. FIAT ANSALDO *TANKETTE*

In the spring of 1932, the Italian-Hungarian Armament Committee provided an original Carden-Lloyd *tankette* to the Hungarian Army. The tank was dismantled and delivered to Hungary as a machinery parts, and the HTI technicians assembled the vehicle without any structural or assembly drawings. The Carden-Lloyd *tankette* was not found to be combat-technically suitable by Hungarian experts.

Despite this, the military leadership saw the acquisition of *tankettes* as an entry type for the development of armoured troops. The relatively low price and running costs allowed for mass procurement, which could create an opportunity to start individual and formation training in bigger scale. For Hungary, the available armoured vehicle on the market at the time was the Italian CV33/35 *tankettes*.

In 1933, the Italian-Hungarian Armament Committee agreed on the introduction of the CV33 *tankette*. In June 1934, the Italians presented in Hungary an improved version of the Carden-Lloyd *tankette*, the CV33 (Caro Veloce - fast tank). The vehicle met the technical and combat requirements excellently and won the approval of the Hungarian side.

According to HTI's assessment, the positive features of the Ansaldo tankett will not be surpassed in the next 4-5 years. This proved to be wrong, but may explain why the next Hungarian tank had to wait five years to enter into the service.

▲ Summer 1939, Hungarian troops parade in Kassa (Kosice), FIAT 3000 light tanks are transported on two-wheeled trailers, pulled by a heavy truck. (Author collection)

▲ The CV33/35 tanks were named by Hungarians 35 M. FIAT-Ansaldo, with a three-digit number plate starting with a capital H. (Author collection)

▼ The light tanks were organised into tank companies, officially called automobile companies, as tanks were banned by the peace treaty at the time. These Ansaldo belonged to the tank company of the 2nd Cavalry Brigade, which prepared for the occupation of Subcarpathia (Carpathia-Ukraine) in March 1939, with the white triangle unit insignia. (Author collection)

In 1935, the Hungarian Army ordered 62 CV33 tanks, which they called *tankettes*, from the Turin company for the first time. The first FIAT Ansaldo *tankettes*, known as 35 M. *tankettes*, arrived in Hungary in September 1935 under the flimsy name of agricultural tractors. A further 67 unarmed CV35s were delivered in March 1936. By the end of 1936, the Hungarian army already had a total of 151 Ansaldo *tankettes*. With the Ansaldos, two Italian training officers also arrived in Hajmáskér in order to help the Hungarian managers in the operation and maintenance of the vehicles.

The 13.5-8.5 mm and 6 mm *tankette* armour protected the crew from small arms and shrapnel. The original Italian 6.5 mm machine gun was not suitable for the Hungarian army, neither because of its size nor other technical characteristics. The 8mm machine gun 07/31 M. Schwarzlose used in the Hungarian army was considered good, but the size and low rate of fire of the weapon made it unsuitable for installation in *tankettes*. Finally, the air-cooled 8 mm Gebauer twin machine gun was installed in the vehicle as a 34/A.M. machine gun for tanks. The twin machine guns were fed by 25-round top-loading banana clips. The machine gun was installed in a Hungarian-designed turret. The turret was originally developed for the Hungarian V-3 experimental tank, adding 60 kg of weight, but allowing vertical movement of the machine gun.

▲ Crews of the 35 M. *tankettes* eating their meals during the occupation of Subcarpathia in March 1939. The crew wears the two-piece leather protective suit designed for armoured personnel and motorcyclists. (Author collection)

▲ Fiat 35M Ansaldo *Tankette*, used by Hungarian troops during military operation to reoccupy Trans-Carpathian territories. The operation took place during the spring of 1939, and the distinguishing mark at the time was the white triangle.

▼ Fiat 35M Ansaldo *Tankette* used by the Galànta gendarmerie battalion in 1944. It was painted dark green, and equipped with the latest Hungarian insignia and the usual insignia of the Mechanised Branch.

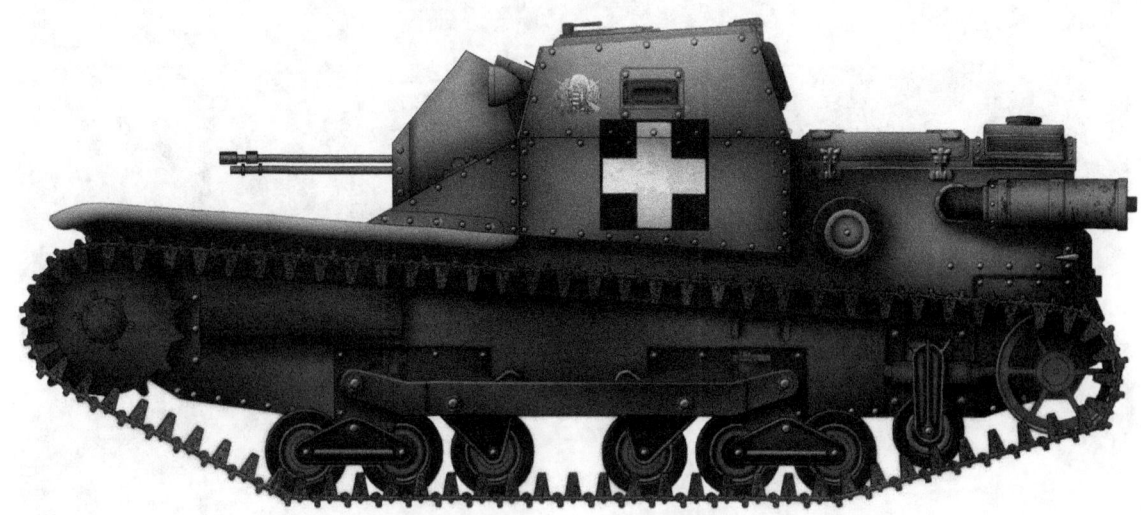

After the successful installation of the weapons, the Military Technical Institute proposed to put into service the Italian tank with Hungarian weapons. It should be noted that, due to the delay in the production of Hungarian machine gun turrets, it was not until 1938 that all the *tankettes* were armed.

However, there were a number of problems with the construction of the vehicle, including poor visibility (it was almost impossible for the driver to see to the rear), which left the vehicle unprotected from the rear; the fragility of the running gear, caused by its complexity and the tendency of the rubber-tired rollers to fail; and the poor quality of the track pads, which caused the pads to stretch and could only be repaired by complete replacement.

In 1937, Italy provided a flamethrower version of the Ansaldo *tankettes* for testing. The machine gun was replaced by a flame thrower, and the ignition fluid was connected to the vehicle by a two-wheel trailer. The test was carried out by the 101st Chemical Warfare Battalion from Piliscsaba. The troops recommended to put in service five vehicles with flamethrowers, but due to lack of funds this was not done. However, the Italian test vehicle remained in Hungary and the Chemical Warfare Battalion received nine more standard Ansaldo with trailers as armoured smoke generator vehicles.

The 1939 operations in Transcarpathia showed that the 35 M. FIAT-Ansaldo *tankettes* had limited technical capabilities, firepower, armour protection and mobility. The track links were quickly worn out, and efforts were made to make up for the shortfall by reordering from Italy and manufacturing domestically.

▲ *Tankette* 35 M. FIAT-Ansaldo, registration plate H-200, belonging to the Non-Commissioned Officers School, painted in three-tone camouflage, with the NCO School unit insignia and, next to the visor slit, the insignia of the Mechanised Branch. (Author collection)

▲ Fiat 35 M. Ansaldo *Tankette* of the 1st Reconnaissance Battalion in 1939. It was painted in the classic Hungarian tricolour. As a distinguishing mark of the unit it had a large white lightning bolt unit sign and the Mechanised Branch insignia.

▼ Fiat 35 M. Ansaldo *Tankette*, used by Hungarian troops during the reconquest of Transylvania, in 1940. It belonged to the 1. Reconnaissance Battalion, it had the Maltese cross military insignia and the Company sign of skull with bones.

Experiments were carried out to strengthen the armament of the *tankettes*, to mount them in a rotating turret. The HTI investigated the replacement one of the twin barrel gun with a 12,7mm barrel. Planes was developed to mount the weapons in a rotating turret and increase the firepower with 20mm anti-tank rifle. These were rejected because of the increase in weight and the general obsolescence of vehicles. Experts already considered the use of the 12,7mm heavy machine gun to be "over-armed".

Finally, as a Hungarian development, for better visibility and observation, a command dome was built over the gunnery position on some of the Ansaldos. 45 tanks were rebuilt, so that in principle all *tankette* platoons had vehicles with observation dome for the commander and the deputy commander.

When the Italian side proposed the procurement of the *tankettes*, it was suggested to buy a truck for transporting tanks and trailers/trolleys, which

▲ The Hungarians attempted to modernise the Ansaldo *tankette* by improving observation with an elevated commander's dome built above the gunner's seat, but in fact did not improve the vehicle's combat value. The H-167 crossing a 33 M. Hungarian military bridge over a Romanian anti-tank ditch during the occupation of Transylvania in September 1940. (Author collection)

In the small photo above: the Hungarian 8 mm 34/37 M. Gebauer twin machine gun, placed in the turret designed for the Hungarian Army to house the machine guns of the Ansaldo *tankettes*. However, the machine guns were fed by a type of 25-round magazine that soon proved insufficient. (Service Manual)

▲ Fiat 35 M. Ansaldo *Tankette* used by the State Police forces. It was entirely painted dark blue. Plate number RR-125.

▼ Fiat 35 M. Ansaldo *Tankette*, shown here in the version with the commander's observation dome. Tri-colour camouflage, the tankette had the octogonal military insignia and Mechanised insignia. The vehicle's license plate was H-126, used by the 1st Armored Cavalry Battalion in 1941.

would have saved the running gear during the road movements. This was not done due to lack of funds, but based on the experience of the 1938-1939 operations, the troops suggested it. During the occupation of Transylvania, different types were tested. The MÁVAG Rába D-4. typ. 4 tons tractor with a two-axle tank transport trailer. Weiss Manfréd Rt's three-axle Ford truck with a two-wheeled transport trailer. The Rába truck could carry two Ansalds, one on the flatbed and one on the trailer. Standard Ford trucks were also experimented with, but only as a stop-gap solution on built-up roads, because their 2.5-tonne capacity was exceeded by the Ansaldo's 3.2-tonne weight.

Finally, the Hungarian military leadership decided that the concept of the *tankettes* had been overtaken by the rapid development of military technology and was therefore doomed to extinction, and that it was not worth spending money on modernising them.

▲ A fine specimen of 35 M. FIAT-Ansaldo *tankette* with three-tone camouflage and large white unit insignia with skull and bones, no military insignia appears yet painted. Crew member wears 35 M. dark brown leather protective suit. Photo colored by Deak Tamas courtesy. (Author collection)

Small photo: Each bicycle battalion had a *tankette* platoon with six 35 M. *tankettes*. These vehicles belonged to the 14th Bicycle Battalion with the unit insignia of a white skull and dagger on the left rear plate. (Author collection)

▲ Fiat CV35 Ansaldo *Tankette* in flamethrower version. Italy sent a sample of it for testing and it was delivered in the typical sandy yellow desert camouflage.

TANKETTE UNITS OF THE HUNGARIAN ARMY

In the early 1930s, *tankettes* basically considered suitable for two tasks. They could be used in direct support of the attacking infantry as self-propelled, armoured machine-gun-carrying vehicles, or they could be used for reconnaissance and support tasks in the framework of fast-moving units. In addition, because of their numbers, the small vehicles were also suitable for training personnel and for carrying out combat and unit exercises.

Due to the arrival of Ansaldo *tankettes*, the organisation of the armoured vehicle troops has also changed. A part of the *tankettes* were subordinated to the existing seven mixed brigades to form seven *Tankette* Companies under the name of "Motor Vehicle Companies". This organisational concept was only implemented on paper. The incoming *tankettes* were brought together at Hajmáskér and Örkénytábor, where a training unit was set up under the command and control of the Experimental Motorised Group and the RUISK Armoured Vehicle Group.

According to the report of 20 April 1936, 96 tanks were stored in Hajmáskér and 54 in Örkénytábor. The war organization of the *Tankette* Company counted on 20 *tankettes*, divided into three platoons, with 6-6 vehicles per platoon. From the point of view of combat capability, it should be mentioned that the Hungarian armament and turrets designed for the *tankettes* were not installed on all vehicles until 1938.

▲ Because of the weakness and fragility of the track system, Ansaldo *tankettes* had to be transported by trucks, or by special trailers, but the Hungarians did not have any suitable ones (Ford trucks could carry only 2.5 tons and *tankettes* were heavier). In the image, an Ansaldo tank with a observation dome for the commander is transported by a Ford truck, but being unsuitable, it gets stuck on a dirt road in Transylvania. (Fortepan)

▲ The crew of the Ansaldo stands at attention, the first man, a junior NCO, performed the duties of gunner/commander respectively, the second was the driver. The second vehicle behind the first has the unit's large white sign with skull and bones. (Author collection)

According to the order of battle planned as of 1 October 1936, consisted of the following elements:

- One-one Motor Vehicle Company was subordinated to the mixed brigades, for training purposes the 1st-4th Companies were concentrated in Hajmáskér and the 5th -7th Companies in Örkénytábor.
- The order of battle of the Motor Vehicles Companies consisted of the company staff, two tank platoons and the supply section. Its complement consisted of 3 officers, 4 non-commissioned officers, 16 commissioned officers and 36 privates, and its equipment included 1 small command car, 2 3-ton trucks (ammunition, fuel and ammunition carriers), 1 R-7 radio car, 2 motorcycles, 6 small trucks and 1 training car.
- The Armoured Vehicle Training Battalion of the Hajmáskér Experimental Motorised Group consisted of an Armoured Vehicle Company (1-1 armoured car and tank platoon) and two *tankettes* companies assigned for training purposes only, whose combat vehicles were the FIAT-Ansaldo of the 1st to 4th Motor Vehicle Companies.

Already from the experience of the 1938 exercises, the inspector of the mobile troops found 35 M. *tankettes* only partially suitable for their basic combat tasks (movement security, reconnaissance, and liaison), mainly in cooperation with the Hussars and the bicycle battalions.

In 1938 the newly created motorised brigades each had one (armoured) reconnaissance battalion. The Reconnaissance Battalion of the 2nd Motorised Brigade was the first true armour unit of the Hungarian Army with one – one armoured car, *tankette* and motorised rifle company. The strength of the unit was based on the 3rd and 4th *Tankette* Companies and on the armoured cars of the Experimental Motorised Group. The cavalry brigades also received one-one *tankette* company.

Later, the armoured units of the cavalry brigades were enlarged to battalion size unit, similar to the reconnaissance battalions of the motorised brigades, consisting of one company each of light tanks (38 M. Toldi), *tankettes* (35 M. FIAT Ansaldo) and armoured cars (39 M. Csaba). The companies had 16 vehicles; three platoons each with 5 armoured vehicles plus the company commander's vehicle. By 1940, the Army had four armoured battalions, two-two reconnaissance and armoured cavalry ones. Due to the reorganisation in 1941, the *tankettes* were grouped into the armoured cavalry battalions.

The cavalry brigades had one armoured battalion with one armoured car company (16 x 39. M Csaba) and two *tankette* companies (36 x 35 M. FIAT Ansaldo). The *tankette* companies were reinforced by one 38 M. Toldi light tank platoon. The six bicycle battalions (10th, 12th, 13th, 14th, 15th, 16th) subordinated to the Mobile Corps also had a *tankette* platoon with six-six 35 M. FIAT Ansaldo *tankettes*.

▲ An Ansaldo *tankette* with observation dome transported by rail on a flat car in 1941. Because of the size of the vehicle, fuel drums were stored next to the 35 M. The young ensign was probably the platoon commander, while in the driver's seat was an reserve officer candidate. (Author collection)

▲ Ansaldo filmed during the summer of 1941 in Ukraine, the vehicles already had octagonal military insignia painted on the four sides of the vehicle, with a lion or wolf's head insignia, probably belonging to one of the bycicle battalions. (Author collection)

▼ Nice picture showing an entire company of Ansaldo *tankette* in a moment of rest during the operation in Transylvania, wearing the Maltese cross military insignia. (Muijzer)

OPERATIONAL HISTORY OF THE ANSALDO TANKETTES IN HUNGARY

Following the Vienna Arbitrage, Hungarian troops peacefully occupied Upper-Hungary from 5 to 10 of November 1938. Four infantry corps (former mixed brigades), I, II, VI, VII, took part in this mission with their *tankette* and cavalry companies, and cyclist battalions.

The FIAT Ansaldo *tankettes* took part in the operation in Trans-Carpathian Ukraine, in 1939. That time, the 2nd Reconnaissance Battalion had one tankett company with 18 x 35 M. FIAT Ansaldo *tankettes*, the light tank company had five FIAT 3000 light tank and the armoured car company had one Corssley, two Vickers armoured cars plus four training vehicles.

The operations started on 14 March 1939, the *tankette* platoon of the 12th Bicycle Battalion, was commanded by 1st Lieutenant Tamás Fráter. He led the advance of his battalion to take a small village, Őrhegyalja. He surprised the defenders, and put out of action a Slovak machine gun with the twin machine guns of his 35 M. FIAT Ansaldos.

The *tankettes* of the reconnaissance and armoured cavalry battalions also participated in the occupation of Transylvania in September 1940. The mountainous terrain worn down the FIAT Ansaldo *tankettes*. Some cases the *tankettes* were drawn by oxen, to overcome the mountain passes. After the operation factory overhaul was performed on almost all vehicles, due to the mechanical wear and brake downs.

▲ After the operation in Ukraine, 100 percent of the Ansaldos needed overhaul at the Military Automobile Depot, plus due to poor performance they were also withdrawn from combat units. (Fortepan)

▲ In this original color image, *tankettes* with the circular cross milirary insignia belonged to the 2. Reconnaissance Battalion are seen making their entrance into a Transylvanian town that had just been liberated by Hungarian forces. (Fortepan)

The *tankette* companies took part in the short but intense operation of the Yugoslavian Campaign. The Ansaldo *tankettes* had no casualties but frequent break downs were common.

During the Soviet Campaign in 1941, an operational group was formed to carry out the military activity against the Red Army, commanded by Lieutenant General Ferenc Szombathelyi, and consisted of the VIII. Corps (1st Mountain Brigade and 8th Frontier Guard Brigade) and the Mobile Corps. The Mobile Corps was led by Major General Béla dálnoki Miklós and comprised of three brigades: the 1st and 2nd Motorised Rifle and 1st Cavalry Brigades.

The 1st Cavalry Armoured Battalion had one armoured car company (16 x 39 M. Csabas armoured cars), and two *tankette* companies (9 x 38 M. Toldi light tanks and 36 x 35 M. FIAT Ansaldo *tankettes*). Each *tankette* company had three *tankette* platoons (6 x 35 M. Ansaldo *tankettes* each), and one light tank platoon (4 x 38 M. Toldi light tank). The remaining one 38. M Toldi light tank was with the battalion staff. Colonel Ferenc Révhegyi commanded the 1st Armoured Cavalry Battalion during the operation in Ukraine, on 21 August Lieutenant Colonel László Bercsényi took over the command of the depleted 1st Armoured Cavalry Battalion from Colonel Ferenc Révhegyi. The cavalry brigade had two and each motorised brigade had one bicycle battalion. The four bicycle battalions, 10th, 12th, 13th, 14th had one-one *tankette* platoons with six Ansaldo *tankettes* each, for a total of 24.

Most of the Ansaldo *tankettes* suffered mechanical break downs due to the difficult terrain and weather. Due to the large number of mechanical problems, civilian technician groups were organised and sent to the front from the Manfred Weiss, Ganz, and MAVAG Factories on July 18. A separate group was organised to deal with the 30 mechanically broken-down Ansaldos.

On 27 July the *tankette* companies of the 1st Armoured Cavalry Battalion was deployed in the direction of Budy to halt the attacking Soviet troops, which counter attacked the Hungarian units. The weather was rainy and the terrain wet and muddy. During this action, according to personal memories the commander of attacking Ansaldos reported to the battalion commander that the terrain is not suitable for attack, but he was challenged by Colonel Révhegyi as a coward. He replied back: *"Order confirmed we are going to die"*

2nd *Tankette* Company of the 1st Armoured Cavalry Battalion with 18 Ansaldo advanced against the enemy at Gordievka, the wet terrain and the heavy undergrowth blocked the advancing *tankettes*, the supporting bicycle platoon of the 14th Bicycle Battalion under the command of Lieutenant Zoltán Kékes separated from the *tankettes*. The bogged down *tankette* company came under heavy enemy artillery and small arms fire. The engines of the FIAT Ansaldos were prone to stalling. The *tankettes'* engine had to be restarted manually, from outside of the vehicle. This meant that the driver had to leave the vehicle, even whilst on the battlefield, to try to start the engine. The drivers left the tanks to restart the halted engines and were killed by infantry and sniper fire. Lieutenant Ferenc Pinezich, commander of the 2nd Company desperately fired with his twin machine gun of his Ansaldo, when he got a direct mortal hit in his *tankette* and died. A platoon commander of the company; Lieutenant Lajos Zomborszky was also killed. Posthumously they were decorated with the Hungarian Knight Cross with swords.

Out of the eighteen 35 M. FIAT Ansaldo 12 and some of their crews were killed in this way. Only one platoon survived, because the platoon commander recognised the danger and turned back in time. At the end of the battle, the 1st Company had six 35 M. FIAT Ansaldos remaining from its original 11.

▲ An Italian flamethrower tank was tested in Hungary and then left in the country. Some Hungarian Ansaldos were also equipped with smoke generator trailers at the 101st Chemical Warfare Battalion. (Author collection)

▲ Around 1944, the Mobile Reserve of the Hungarian State Police received ten Ansaldos manned by policemen, all cars were painted dark blue and armed with a single light machine gun. (MTI)

▼ In the late 1930s, the Italians also became interested in the Hungarian V-3 light tank and tested it. The V-3 was equipped with a wheeld-track system, pictured Italian technical and military personnel posing on the tank from which they removed the tracks. (Sarhidai)

This incident highlighted the poor performance of the Ansaldo in battle and marked the end of its military career. The Ansaldo *tankettes* were officially deleted from the combat vehicles of the Army, relegated to training vehicles. After the withdrawal of the 35 M. Ansaldos from active duty, ten each of the remaining vehicles were given to the Police, Gendarmerie and to the Croatian Forces. These were supplied without armaments, and the new owners had to install any weapons.

101st Motorised Chemical Warfare Battalion

The 101st Motorised Chemical Warfare Battalion was organised in 1938, and had a platoon of 35 M. Ansaldos. The task of this battalion was to perform smoke screen and flame throwing activities, and to use combat gases and gas counter-measures against the enemy. Only two 35 M. Ansaldos were equipped with trolleys for transporting smoke screen generators or flamethrower liquid, but neither saw any action.

Gendarmerie

In 1942 a gendarmerie battalion was formed at Galánta, which was responsible for internal security (against armed riots); it had three rifle companies, one bicycle company, one heavy weapons company and one armoured company. The 35 M. Ansaldos were transferred to this unit. In 1944 the gendarmerie armoured company had 12 Ansaldo *tankettes* and one platoon of 39 M. Csaba armoured cars. The police and gendarmerie Ansaldos were deployed and destroyed during the siege of Budapest in 1944/1945.

Police forces

As of 1942, the mobile reserve of the State Police was also equipped with armoured vehicles. An armoured group of State Police was organised with ten 35 M. Ansaldo *tankettes* and two (or five) 39 M. Csaba armoured cars and a special storm detachment to keep internal order in the capital. The 35 M. Ansaldos were equipped with one 31 M. light machine-gun instead of the military equipment.

▲ The *swan song* of the Ansaldo *tankettes* was the siege of Budapest, where they were deployed by police and gendarmes and easily knocked out by Soviet troops. (Author collection)

▲ A Hungarian Ansaldo *tankette* engaged in Ukraine. Note the typical Italian-model *tankette* headgear. Photo colored by Deak Tamas courtesy. (War Correspondent Company)

▼ Hungarian military insignia From right to left 1-4 different tankette companies, NCO School, 1. Reconnaissance Battalion, tankette company, 101. C.hemical Warfare Battalion, 2. Reconaissance, 1. Armoured Cavalry Battalion.

A. WWI sign, Romfell armoured car

B. 1919, Büssing-Fross armoured car

C. 1938, nr.102 armoured train.

D. 1st Reconnaissance Battalion 1940.

E. 1st Reconnaissance Battalion 1940.

F. 1st Reconnaissance Battalion 1940.

G. 1st Reconnaissance Battalion 1940.

H. 2nd Reconnaissance Battalion 1940.

I. Mobile Training Camp

J. 2nd Armoured Cavalry Battalion 1940.

K. Octogonal military sign 1941-42

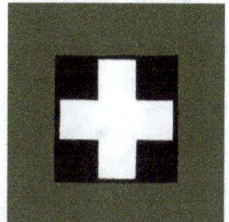
L. Late war military sign 1942-45

Mechanised Branch's Sign (decal)

▲ Hungarian military insignia for tanks and military vehicles. Source by Huns on wheels.

FURTHER PROJECTS

Medium tanks

In September 1937, the Italians shown interest of testing the Hungarian V-4 medium tank. The crew of three version was delivered to Italy. It was tested, but did not meet the expectations and returned only on 5 October 1942.

The Hungarians recognised the importance of the medium and heavy tanks in the modern, mobile warfare. But the Hungarian military industry was unable to offer the suitable tanks. The only Hungarian developed V-4 tank was outdated by that time. The Hungarian experts turned towards foreign procurements. The acquisition and the purchase of licensing rights were also under consideration.

The Italians did not have the appropriate types either, but the Italian-Hungarian Armament Committee held a meeting in the summer of 1939, which gave the Hungarian side the opportunity to get acquainted with Italian tank types. In Genoa, at the Ansaldo Works, Colonel János Vértessy and Captain Sándor Bartholomeidesz were able to study the offered M11/39 and M13/40 medium tanks. These vehicles did not meet Hungarian expectations, the M11/39 tank was developed on the basis of the experiences of the Ethiopian war. The technical parameters of the M.13/40 tank did not exceed those of the Skoda T-21.

Assault guns

According some memoires, the Hungarians visited the Italian factory producing the Semovente assault gun, somewhere in 1942. This visit inspired the Hungarians to build their home designed assault artillery vehicles, the Zrínyi. At least we have to note that both assault artillery vehicles were gap-stop weapons, built on the basis of the existing, home produced hull of a medium tank with the available artillery barrels. In Italy it was the Semovente assault artillery vehicles and in Hungary the 40/43 M. Zrínyi assault howitzers.

▲ Original color photo of the 1940 occupation of Transylvania with 35 M. tankette on parade. (MTI)

▲ The Hungarian Straussler V-4 medium tank that aroused some interest in the Italian General Staff. Col. Deak Tamas.

▼ Preserved model of CV35 of Hungarian origin displayed in Belgrade, note the titpic Hungarian machine gun dome wider than the original Italian equivalents!

▲ ▼ Hungarian 35 M. *tankette* with commander's dome at Kubinka Tank Museum painted in Italian colors.

▲ Hungarian 35 M. tank with commander's dome in Kubinka Tank Museum with Italian colors.
▼ Hungarian CV35 exhibited in Belgrade.

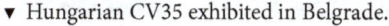

▲▼ The Hungarian-designed dome for the twin-machine gun, also of Hungarian manufacture. Collection of the Hungarian Military Museum courtesy.

▲▼ More images related to the Hungarian Ansaldo *tankette* preserved in Belgrade.

▲ Hungarian commander's Ansaldo in Kubinka painted with Italian desert sand colors.

▼ Hungarian Ansaldo in Belgrade with spotted sand color camouflage.

▲▼ Hungarian commander's Ansaldo in Kubinka painted with Italian desert sand colors.

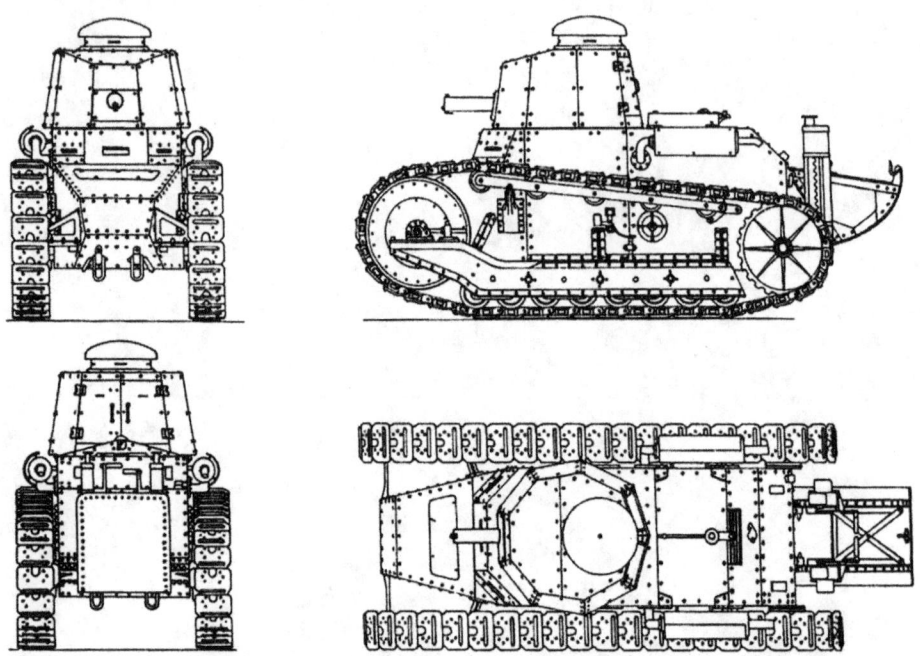

▲ Four views of the FIAT 3000 light tank also supplied to the Hungarian armed forces. (Benczur)

▼ Four views of the 35 M. FIAT-Ansaldo *tankette* in the Hungarian version with commander's dome. (Bajtos)

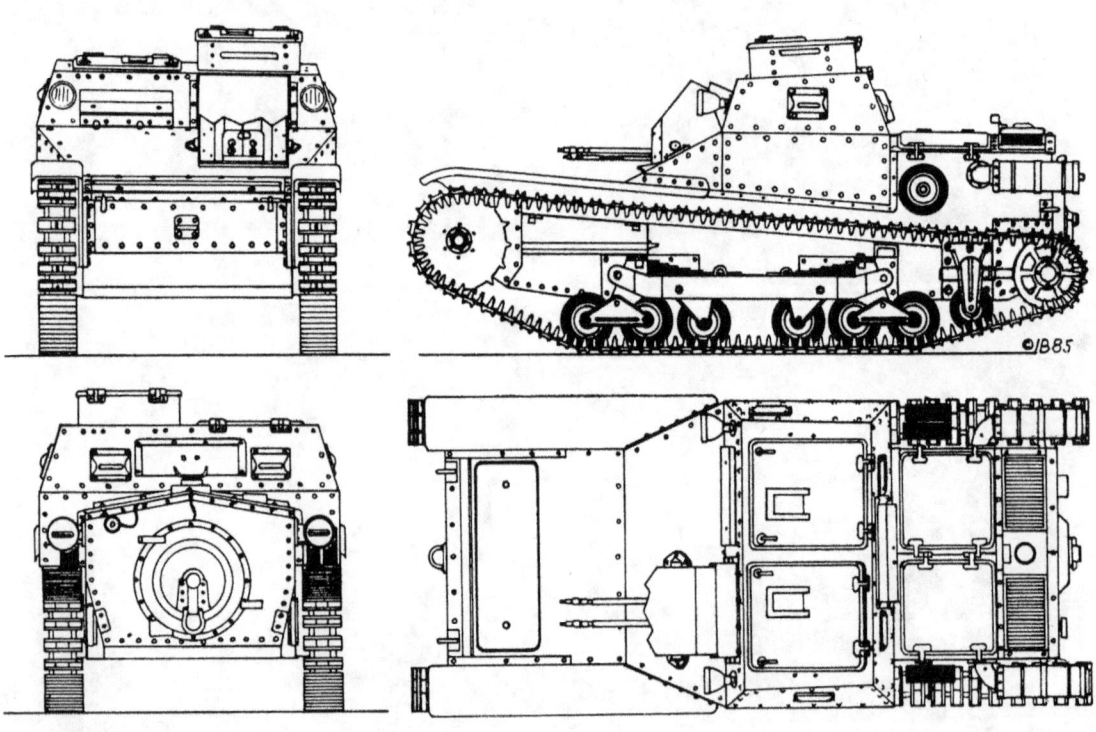

ITALIAN VEHICLES IN THE HUNGARIAN ARMY

The Hungarian purchased command cars, trucks, artillery tractors, special vehicles and motorcycles from Italy from the 30s to mid-40s. Between 1938 and 1944 bout 800 military cars and trucks plus 700 motorcycles arrived to Hungary.

SMALL CARS

FIAT 508 small car
In 1933 FIAT 508M small cars were purchased, the exact numbers not yet known.

FIAT 508 C 1100 small car
The FIAT 508 C 1100 small, four-seater command car arrived in 1938, 103 cars were purchased.

Fiat Torpedo Militare small command car
In early June 1939, the Fiat 508 Coloniale 1100 passenger cars was replaced by Fiat Torpedo Militare small command car. According to the Hungarian Military archive 219 cars were ordered. In three different purchase credit (76+24+14), in total 114 were purchased. By the end of 1939, all of them had arrived in colonial brown with one spare wheel. Although the model was not an off-road vehicle, it handled well on both paved and dirt roads. Primarily the newly organized anti-aircraft artillery battalions, the reconnaissance battalions received the type.

▲ The civilian version of the FIAT 508 Topolino parked next to the prototype of the AC. I. designed by Nicolas Straussler in the early 1930s. (Fortepan)

▲ FIAT 508 M Spider small command car in the summer of 1939 in Subcarpathia. (Fortepan)

Medium cars
FIAT 520 F.4 medium car
In 1933 a few FIAT 520 F.4 medium cars were purchased in 1933.

Large cars
FIAT 2F large car
In 1929, some FIAT 2F large car was delivered to the Hungarian Army.

FIAT 512 large car
Unknown number of FIAT 512 large car arrived in 1931 to Hungary.

FIAT 525 N large car
FIAT 525 N large car landed in 1932.

▲ Staff car, FIAT Ballila 508 M painted dark olive green with the Mechanised Branch metal insignia attached to the door. The driver had the driving insignia, a metal winged wheel, on his sleeve. (Fortepan)

▲ FIAT staff car with the metal insignia of the Mechanized Branch attached to the door in the early 1930s. (Author collection)

▼ Command staff car, FIAT 508 M with Mechanized Branch sticker and unit insignia. (Author collection)

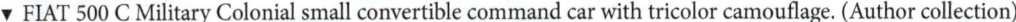

▲ FIAT 500 C Military Colonial small convertible car with two officers in 1941, three-tone camouflage and Mechanized Branch sticker visible on door. (Fortepan)

▼ FIAT 500 C Military Colonial small convertible command car with tricolor camouflage. (Author collection)

▲ Romanian and Hungarian officers coordinating troop movements in Transylvania in front of a small FIAT 500 C Military Colonial belonging to the 3rd Motorized Battalion, September 1940. (Fortepan)

▼ FIAT 1100 Military Torpedo, NCO School staff car, with three-tone camouflage, with the school insignia painted in white on both fenders and sides of the vehicle. (Author collection)

▲ FIAT 508 C/1100 Military Torpedo, staff car of the NCO School during the occupation of Transylvania, with three-tone camouflage and white school insignia painted on the right fender. (Author collection)

Small photo: official photograph of the FIAT 1100 Torpedo Militare passenger car from the factory catalog.

▲ Reserve officer cadets of the 101st Automobile Training Regiment posing on their FIAT 15 truck, in mechanic's overalls. (Fortepan)

TRUCKS

FIAT XV 1,5 tons truck

Unknown number of FIAT XV 1,5 tons trucks called by the Hungarians "Tripoli" was purchased by the Army in 1928. Some of them transported the central aiming device for the 5/8 M. anti-aircraft batteries.

FIAT 4. Ts. truck

A small number of 4 tons FIAT 4. Ts. was put into service in 1930.

6M Autocaretta-32 small all-terrain truck

100 Autocarrettes were delivered to Hungarian troops for chemical warfare to transport smoke generators and decontamination equipment. The first vehicles arrived in Hungary in 1940. Although sources speak of 6M Autocarette 32, according to photographic evidence the Hungarians used Autocarette 36.

FIAT Spa Dovunque 2,5 tons all-terrain truck

It was outdated at the beginning of the war, 33 trucks served at the searchlight units, 7 towed the Galileo listening device. The chemical warfare units also got 18 trucks for disinfection and degassing. From 1941 the FIAT Spa trucks were regrouped into the Air Defence units.

38 M. Fiat Spa 38 R 2,5 tons trucks

In 1937 the Hungarians ordered 700 Fiat Spa 38 R 2.5-ton trucks, the number of which delivered is not known, most of them built with workshop superstructures, served at the maintenance subunits of the motorized and armored battalions until the end of the war.

▲ FIAT Spa 38 Dovunque truck leading the 38 M. Botond trucks during the occupation of Transylvania in September 1940. (Fortepan)

▲ OM Autocarretta 36 belonging to the 101st Chemical Warfare Battalion. Classic green coloring with Mechanised Branch sticker.

▼ OM Autocarretta 36 in Hungarian three-tone camouflage version: green, light yellow and dark brown always with Mechanised Branch sticker.

▲ OM Autocarretta 36 belonging to the 101st Chemical Warfare Battalion while laying a smoke screen during an exercise in 1940.
Small photo: the same department in other exercises.

▼ OM Autocarretta 36 belonging to the 101st Chemical Warfare Battalion, crew wearing gas masks and protective suits, the truck was carrying a smoke generator.

▲ Maintenance of FIAT 15 trucks at the 101st Automobile Training Regiment in 1943 on the banks of the Danube. (Fortepan)

▼ FIAT Spa Dovunque truck belonging to civilian defense troops, the crew wears chemical protective suits and gas masks. The truck appears in typical Hungarian tri-tone camouflage. (MTI)

▲ ▼ FIAT Spa Dovunque truck equipped with 37 M. Galileo searchlight, towing generators during the military parade in honor of King Victor Emmanuel III in Budapest, May 20, 1937. (Fortepan)

▲ FIAT Spa Dovunque truck 38R used to transport troops during training. (Author collection)

▼ Washing the FIAT Spa Dovunque truck 38R that belonged to the 101st Automobile Training Regiment at the Danube River 1943. (Fortepan)

▲ Some of the FIAT Spa Dovunque 38R trucks were converted into workshop vehicles for motorized unit maintenance columns. This vehicle was sent to Ukraine in 1941. (Author collection)

▼ FIAT Spa Dovunque 38R truck during the mobilization of a motorized unit in 1941. (Fortepan)

▲ FIAT Spa Dovunque 38R trucks waiting to be delivered to troops at a temporary depot in Budapest, 1943. (Fortepan)

▼ Hungarian Royal Air Force Isotta Fraschini D70M trucks and trailers that belonged to an air squadron ground service unit in the late 1930s. (Fortepan)

ARTILLERY TRACTORS

28 M. Pavesi artillery tractor

The first Italian Pavesi artillery tractors arrived to Hungary in 1925, 20 were purchased from the first series. Later the Weis Manfréd Factory purchased the licence rights of the Pavesi P4-100 artillery tractor and from 1928 to 1940, 128 28 M. Pavesi artillery tractors produced for the Hungarian Army. Another 103 Pavesi were purchased from Italy in 1930-1931. It was used for towing the 80mm Bofors anti-aircraft guns, the medium howitzers and engineer materials (pontoons, bridging materials).

32 M. Breda artillery tractors

For towing the heavy artillery pieces 104 Breda heavy artillery tractors was purchased. 16 tractors arrived in 1937-1938, another 86 in 1940. Although, the 32 M. Breda tractors were obsolete, but remained in Hungarian service at the heavy artillery units, towing the 210mm howitzers and the 305mm heavy mortars until 1944.

▲ The Pavesi tractor, a versatile vehicle, was also used by the Engineer Corps troops to transport heavy material. (Fortepan)

▲ The Pavesi artillery tractor entered in the Hungarian Army service under the model name 28 M. painted in dark-olive gree with Mechanised Branch insignia.

▲ The first 20 Pavesi P4/100 artillery tractors arrived in Hungary in 1925. (Author collection)

▼ Pavesi artillery tractors were put into service with the Hungarian Army under the new local designation of 28 M artillery tractors. (Author collection)

▲ The Pavesi tractor's ability to traverse fields and natural obstacles was well demonstrated, as can be seen from the image, but nevertheless by the beginning of the war the vehicle had already proven to be slow and obsolete. (Fortepan)

▼ The main role of the Pavesi artillery tractors was to tow the 150 mm 31 M medium howitzers. The photo was taken in the summer of 1942 on the Don River, the artillery tractor pulling not only the howitzer in one unit, but also the ammunition train. (Fortepan)

▲ The open cabin of 28 M. Pavesi was certainly not ideal in winter conditions. (Fortepan)
▼ Medium 150 mm howitzers were normally transported in two units, the gun-carrieg and the barrel pulled by Pavesi tractors, as seen in this photo, taken during the occupation of Transylvania. (Fortepan)

▲ Pavesi tractor towing the barrel section of a medium howitzer during a military parade. (MTI)

▼ Military parade for the King of Italy held on May 20, 1937, Bofors anti-aircraft guns pulled by Pavesi tractors passing the VIP grandstand. (Fortepan)

▲ A Pavesi tractor pulls a Bofors anti-aircraft gun under a triumphal arch erected on the occasion of the reocuption of Transylvania by the Magyar Armed Forces. (Fortepan)

▼ Nice modell of a Pavesi tractor, here in the Hungarian three-tone camouflage version.

▲ The Hungarians modernized some of the old 100 mm howitzers Mod. 14. from World War I, converting them into motorized 14 M/As, also pulled by Pavesi tractors. (Fortepan)

▼ The Hungarian heavy artillery had Breda 32 artillery tractors, designated by the Hungarians as 32 M. Breda tractors. In this photo, a heavy artillery battalion is transported by train to the eastern front in 1942, the unit's insignia was painted on the driver's cab panel. (War Correspondent Company)

▲ The supply of spare parts for foreign vehicles was often problematic. In this photo, spare parts for Breda and Isotta vehicles are stored at the Central Army Automobile Depot in Mátyásföld, Budapest, in 1943. (Fortepan)

▲ The Breda artillery tractor entered in the Hungarian army under the model name 32 M. Generally ipainted in dar-olive green with Mechanised Branch insignia.

▲ The old 305 mm Skoda mortar was also transported in separate units, with the Breda tractor pulling the heavy mortar barrel, as seen in the photo during the occupation of Transylvania in September 1940. (Fortepan)

▼ After the siege of Budapest ended, a burned Breda tractor and a knocked out 40/43 M. Zrínyi assault howitzer are visible at the Castle. (Fortepan)

▲ Bianchi 500M motorcycle used by dispatch riders, this one belonged to the 103rd Heavy Artillery Battalion, and the picture is from 1940-1941. (Author collection)

▼ Gilera motorcycle, also used by dispatch riders in the late 1930s and early 1940s. (Factory catalogue)

MOTORCYCLES

Bianchi 500M motorcycle

The Hungarian Army tried to remedy the shortage of motorcycles by buying new ones. In the framework of the Italian-Hungarian military cooperation. 80 Bianchi 500M (M = militare) of 1937 production arrived in Hungary, and the domestic production of these motorcycles was also considered. Negotiations for the purchase of the licence were broken off because the Italian side had set a high production number. The type did not prove a success with the troops, with frequent breakages due to material defects.

Gilera 500 motorcycles

In 1936 Gilera solo motorcycles were purchased by the Hungarian Army, 400 were delivered until 1940, used by the dispatch riders.

Gilera Marte 500 side-car motorcycles

The Hungarian military delegation in Rome in March 1943 inspected the Gilera Marte sidecar motorcycle used by the Italian Army. Original 1000 ordered, due to the shortage of raw materials, the order was reduced to 300 units. The test vehicles arrived in Mátyásföld in July 1943, at the Military Automobile Depot. After being commissioned and number plated, it was sent to the Military Technical Institute for 3 days to check the technical data provided by the factory, and then it was issued to the 15th Bicycle Battalion for a 14-day trial. Even before the trials started, it was clear to the 3/b Department of the MoD - and the

▲ Side view of the Gilera Marte sidecar motorcycle. (Factory catalogue)

▲ Gilera Marte sidecar motorcycles delivered to Hungary in 1943, used by the motorcycle companies of the reconnaissance and cyclist battalions. (Author collection)

▲ Perspective technical drawing of the Gilera Marte sidecar motorcycle. (factory catalogue)

report received from the troop trials confirmed this - that the Gilera Marte 500 with sidecar was only a stopgap solution. According to the summary, "the motorcycle is not suitable for combat use and for transporting 3 people. The department had already noted from the HTI's opinion on the basis of the specification that the motorcycle could only be used as a stop-gap solution, but we still had to order 300 units because no other sidecar motorcycle was available by the end of the year."

The Gileras were expected to be delivered in August 1943, but in fact the delivery took place only on 22 February 1944 and the deliveries began in March, lasting almost the whole year. By 11 October 1944, a total of 265 Gilera 500 sidecar motorcycles had arrived in Budapest, along with 35 crates of spare parts and equipment. Some of the consignments were hit by air raids, returned to the factory for repair and then sent back on the road.

According to the report of the 3rd Motorcycle Company of the 15th Bicycle Battalion, the tested motorcycle was described as reliable and durable, and no engine malfunctions or design faults were found during the test. The HTI has recommended to the Minister of Defence that the Gilera Marte put into service as 43 M. Gilera Marte side-car motorbike.

▲▼ The Italian 210 mm 39 M heavy howitzer was the most important artillery piece to be consigned to the Hungarians, who also provided the rights for a licensed production of it called 39/40 M.

As with many other Magyar army vehicles, the basic coloring was green while the camouflage was the classic three-tone camouflage already seen on tanks and vehicles of all kinds.

ARTILLERY COOPERATION

In the summer of 1939, the first Italian heavy howitzers arrived with ammunition. In the test firings, the Italian shells performed badly. On the advice of the HTI, the foreign procurement was abandoned and completely new Hungarian ones were designed. The resulting Hungarian ammunition was a new addition to the already established and proven 33M ammunition development line.

Despite this, in March 1940, under the pressure of the incipient ammunition shortage, 1,400 fragmentation shells and 5,600 destructive shells were ordered, but by 1941 the full quantity had still not arrived. On impact, the fuse tips of several fragmentation grenades broke off due to a material defect. The 21 cm Csepel ammunition production base was completely lost in the 1944 bombing raids. Therefore, in August the High Command requested 15-20 thousand shells from the Italians, but none of these were ever delivered.

Ammunition for the 5 existing 30.5 cm mortars was also hidden from the Entente's inspection committees. In the period from about 1930 to 1937, these ammunitions were used for training and gunnery. The shells often on impact slipped, broke and did not explode, even on flat ground. Due to the sudden demand for ammunition Italian supply helped. Estimated quantity purchased: 4500-5000 shells. The ammunition was of First World War design. Nevertheless, they were reliable.

On 13 October 1938 (after the failed Hungarian-Czechoslovak negotiations), in view of the tense foreign policy situation, the 3rd a. department of the Ministry of Defence received

▲ One of the most modern weapons in the Hungarian artillery was the Italian 210 mm heavy howitzer 39 M. It was delivered to Hungary from the beginning of 1940. (Author collection)

▲ Later the Hungarians acquired the license for the 39 M heavy howitzer and produced it at the Diósgyőr Gun Factory under the name 39/40 M. It was intended for the artillery units of the field armies and army corps. (Author collection)

▼ The 210 mm heavy howitzers pulled by Breda Mod. 32 tractors in two units, barrel and carriage. Here we see them presented to the public for the first time during the occupation of Transylvania. (Fortepan)

▲ The Hungarian-made heavy howitzer was designated as a 39/40 M. heavy howitzer and served in heavy howitzer battalions. (Author collection)

an order from the III. Directorate for immediate, urgent German and Italian orders. From Italy: (in addition to other ammunition) -10 cm fragmentation grenades -15 cm fragmentation grenades -15 cm fragmentation grenades -15 cm fragmentation grenades -30,5 cm fragmentation grenades - 40,000 pieces - 15,000 pieces - 15,000 pieces - 500 pieces Total value of about 6,800,000 pence, from warehouse delivery. The composition of the orders reflects the expected destruction tasks of the Czechoslovak fortification system, but also shows that the domestic artillery stocks were still severely depleted at that time. But the urgency of the order also had a number of drawbacks. It is true that the Italians supplied cheaper than the domestic factories (by 40-45%) General Henrik Werth, the Chief of the General Staff, based on the 1939 report of the Field Artillery School, ordered that Italian light and medium shells should be used for training purposes. In fact, about 40 % of the Italian ammunition failed to explode during the firing exercises. At the same time, because of their unstable and insufficiently safe operation, he prohibited their use in exercises involving other branches of the armed forces.

The Italian 210mm 35 M heavy howitzer and its license production

According to the expansion of the Hungarian heavy artillery seven heavy artillery battalions (3 batteries/2 howitzers) plus 6 spare one, altogether 48 heavy howitzers should serve by December 1940 in the heavy artillery battalions. The Hungarians favoured the home production under licence rights. They considered the Swedish and Italian howitzers too.

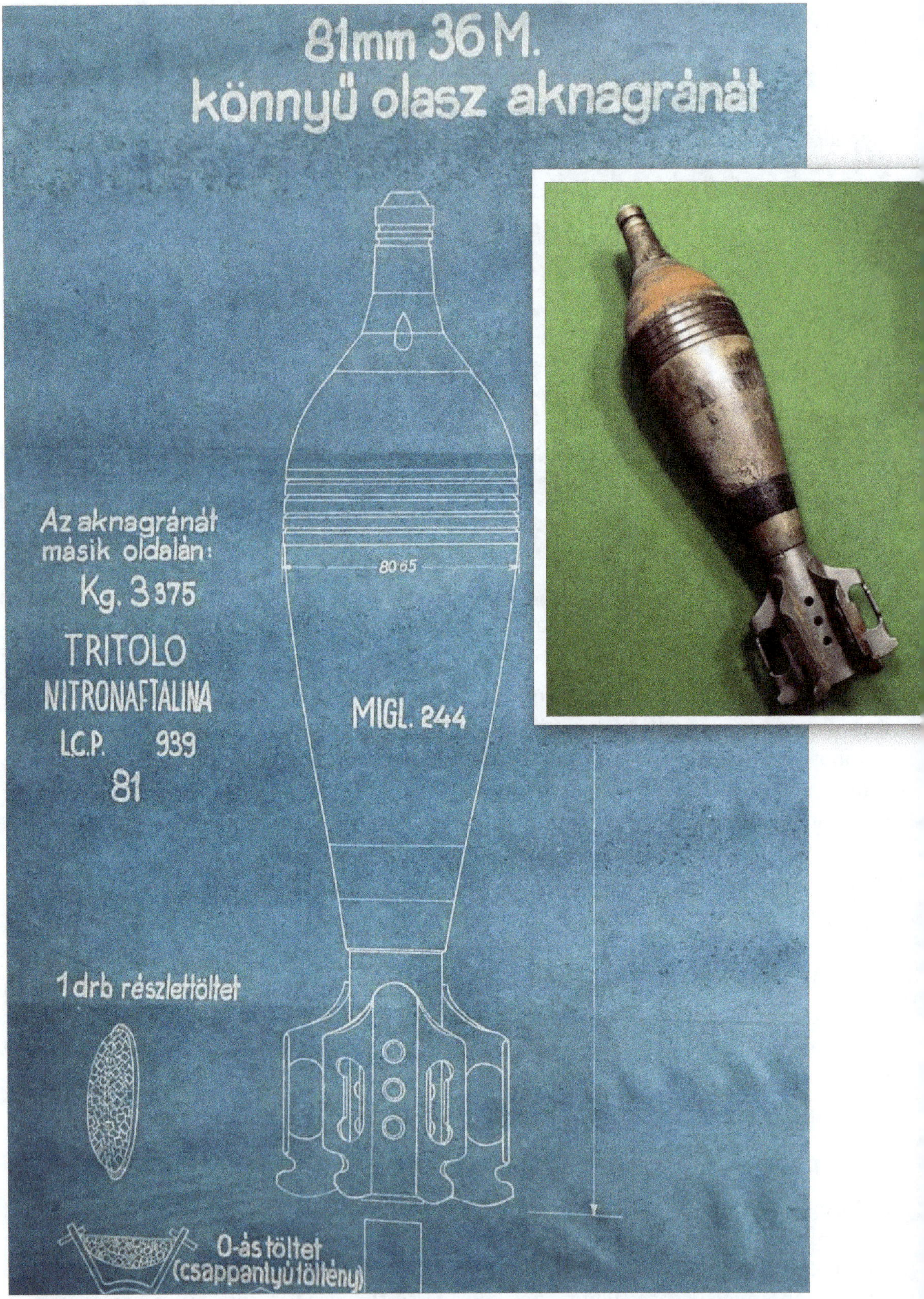

81mm 36 M. könnyű olasz aknagránát

Az aknagránát másik oldalán:
Kg. 3 375
TRITOLO
NITRONAFTALINA
L.C.P. 939
81

MIGL. 244

80·65

1 drb részlettöltet

0-ás töltet
(csappantyú töltény)

▲ Diagram of the 81 mm Italian mortar shell offered for delivery by the Italians to the Hungarian Army. Service manual

Finally the Hungarians chosen the Italian solution, although it was not yet mass produced that time. However, due to the time pressure 8 heavy howitzers were ordered from Italy in 1938. The first, experimental howitzer was sent by the end of the year. Due to the tests some engineering modification had to be performed. Even, the production of the 21 cm heavy howitzers, which took up the considerable capacity of the Diósgyőr gun factory for a long time, was very cumbersome and fraught with many pitfalls. Also, the Italian production was delayed, the first two howitzers were promised in 1939, the remaining six only in 1940. The Hungarians wanted to order six more heavy howitzers, but due the problems in production, the Italians could not guarantee the delivery times. The Hungarians visited the Factory in March 1939, to urge the deliveries. Instead of that, General Caraccino informed the Hungarians that the original 1.870.000 lire price increased to 2.370.000 lire. Finally, six howitzers arrived in late 1939 and further two in January 1940. The first two heavy howitzers were subordinated to 2nd Batteries of the 101st and 102nd Heavy Howitzer Battalions. The delivered 210 mm heavy howitzers were distributed among the 101st and 102nd Heavy Howitzer Battalions. One Italian heavy howitzer was at the disposition of the HTI for further testing in accordance to the development of the home made howitzers.

Nevertheless, in the autumn of 1941 the first 40 M. Hungarian 210mm howitzer was delivered in Diósgyőr, which proved to be considerably more usable than the original version. Together with the 26 gun carriages that were put into service, it was completed during 1942-43. The last pieces were taken out of the role in 1943.

▲ Beautiful view of the 210 mm heavy howitzer preserved in a fort-museum in Italy.

▲▼ Original color photos of the 37 M. Galileo searchlight unit deployed in the woods during an exercise in 1940. (Fortepan)

OTHER EQUIPMENT

34 M. Juhász-Gamma Fire control equipment

During the war one of the best anti-aircraft fire control system was designed by István Juhász and produced by Gamma Factory. The Juhász-Gamma anti-air fire control instrument determining the parameters of airborne targets and the necessary elements for firing. It was the first electromechanically operated analogue computer, internationally renowned for its reliability and accuracy. The Gamma Factory produced over 1000 devices and exported into 16 countries. The Hungarian anti-aircraft artillery only used the 10% of the produced equipments.

The Italians have shown interest. In 1941, 12 (18 pieces according to other sources) were ordered for air defence. On 10 August 1943, the Hungarian MoD blocked all deliveries due to the fall of the Mussolini government. At the end of 1943, the first 4 completed devices were taken over by the Hungarian Army.

Rangefinder

The Hungarians also ordered 1 meter rangefinders from the Italian Galileo Company. The partner company, the Hungarian Gamma Factory reported to the Hungarian MoD that the first 15.20 rangefinders will be ready by July 1940 and the other 25-30 would be finished by August.

▲The antiaircraft artillery had a few 150-cm 37 M. Galileo searchlight. Most served with static antiaircraft artillery units that protected the capital and industrial centers. (Author collection)

Search lights

Until 1932, the Hungarian had no search lights, then one-one 120 cm and 150 cm Galileo searchlights were ordered from Italy with Ronchi eavesdropping device. All together seven searchlight platoons were organised with Italian equipment.

The 37 M. Galileo searchlights were transported on FIAT Spa Dovunque 2,5 tons all-terrain trucks.

Infantry weapons

In 1939, the Cemsa Saronno Factory offered a 81mm mortar to the Hungarian Army, the HTI recommended the testing of the Italian mortar with the range of 3800 meters with 3,4 kilogram and 1600 meters with 6,9 kilogram mortar shells. The 1. department of the Chief of Staff did not recommend it.

In 1940, on the request of the Italian Military Technical Institute the Hungarian counterpart sent one Polish 8mm anti-tank rifle to Italy in August of 1940. Based on the evaluation of the anti-tank rifle, the Italians purchased in large quantity captured Polish wz.35 anti-tank rifles from Germany for their airborne troops. The wz.35 was used by the Italian paratroopers in the Desert.

▲ Another original color photo of the 37 M. Galileo searchlight unit deployed in the woods during an exercise in 1940. (Fortepan)

Flamethrower

Based on the experiences of World War I assault troops, initially the Hungarian light infantry (jaeger battalions and grenadier companies) were trained in the use of World War I Italian flamethrowers. Preparing to recapture lost territories, the Hungarians had to face different types of fortress belts to take down. An experimental assault battalion was organized to test methods and weapons, including flamethrowers. Later, the 101st Chemical Warfare Battalion and Corps engineer battalions were provided with Italian mod. 41 and 43 portable flamethrowers, which were deployed to the Don River in 1942.

▲ The anti-aircraft artillery also had a number of Ronchi listening devices to support the anti-aircraft guns. (Author collection)

▲ Hungarian soldiers posing with an Italian Bersaglier in Dnepropetrovsk, Ukraine, in the fall of 1941. (Fortepan)

▼ Joint checkpoint of Italian Carabinieri and a Hungarian gendarme near the Don River in 1942. (Fortepan)

UNIFORMS & EQUIPMENT

A significant number of different leathers, fabric material was purchased from Italy as well as shirts, blankets, as it was noted earlier.

Crash helmet

One of the most distinctive equipment pieces with Italian origins were the crash helmet for motorcyclist and armoured troops based on the Italian crash helmet. At first civilian motorcycle headgear was used by the armoured troops. This was replaced in 1937 by the Italian-designed 37 M. leather armoured headgear. The headgear consisted of a vulcanised fibre dome, a matching tyre-like insert, a surrounding swell-like padding and a neck guard and ear protection chin strap. The dome was covered with black dyed horsehide and the neck guard was made of sheepskin. The helmet was made in three sizes. The armoured headgear was well-proven and remained in use until the end of the war.

The 38 M. Toldi tanks and 39/40 M. Csaba armoured personnel cars made it necessary to introduce the radio headgear. The Hungarian-developed 39 M. "radio helmet" had a flatter shape and was equipped with earphones which, together with a throat microphone, allowed communication inside and outside the vehicle.

▲ Italian 35M gas mask with canvas case.

▲ Model 41 flamethrower used by Hungarian engineer units during the battles for the bridgehead battles around the Don River in the summer of 1942. Small photo: flamethrower operator wears protective gloves and some sort of protective suit. (Author collection)

▼ Italian-made camouflage tent used by the Hungarian army, with Italian patterns and colors. (Angyal)

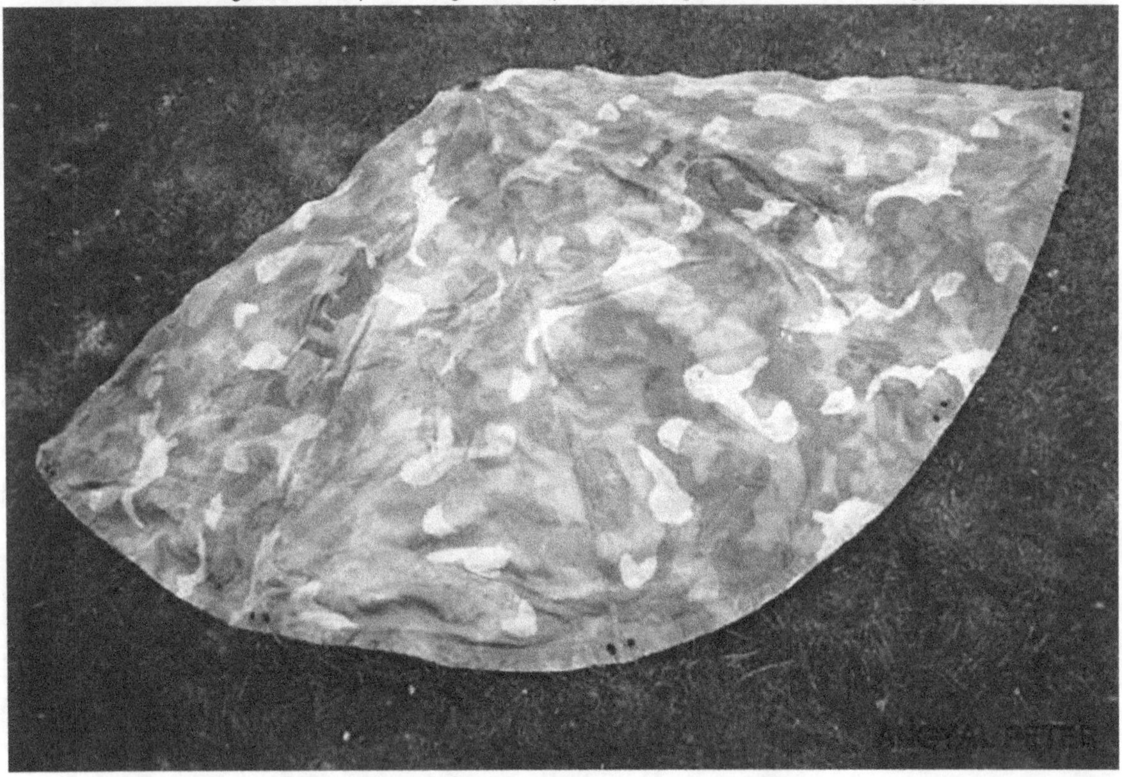

Gasmask

The Italian 35M gas mask had a very similar canvas case than the 34 M. Hungarian. It was developed by the Hungarian Mercure Ltd. in early 30s and put in military service by 1934.

Unknown number of the Italian M30 rubberised chemical suit was in service at the 101st Chemical Warfare Battalion.

Camouflaged half-tent

The Hungarian Army only camouflaged equipment piece was the 38 M. half-tent, rain poncho. The Hungarians ordered Italian half-tent from Italy too. The design of the half-tents made in Italy for the Hungarian order is completely different from the Hungarian made ones, using the original Italian material, with Italian or Hungary pattern camouflage. Another difference is the hole at the top of the tent, which is smaller in cross-section and reinforced with twine instead of metal insert.

Camouflage and markings

The Italian vehicles, aircrafts arrived to Hungary in their distinctive colours/camouflage. Which was later overpainted with the Hungarian three tone (dark olive green - chestnut brown – dirt yellow) or single colour (dark olive green) camouflage.

▲ Flame throws used by Hungarian assault troops in the exercise of breaking through an enemy fortification in 1940, in preparation for a military conflict with Romania. (War Correspondent Company)

▲ Hungarian supply column, probably belonging to the Royal Hungarian Air Force, equipped with Fiat 508 passenger cars and Isotta Fraschini D70M trucks camping at Lake Balaton in 1940. (Author collection)

▼ Isotta Fraschini D70M truck with field kitchens belonging to the catering section of the supply column in 1940. (Author collection)

▲ The Italians ordered some GAMMA-Juhász anti-aircraft fire control machines from Hungary. (Fortepan)
▼ Ronchi listening device used by Hungarian antiaircraft artillery. (Author collection)

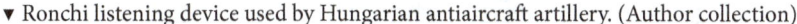

▲ Hungarian motorized and armored troops received the Italian-style leather helmet, named 37 M. protective helmet for armored troops. (Fortepan)

▼ General Italo Gariboldi, commander of the Italian 8th Army, visits Colonel General Gusztáv Jány, commander of the Hungarian 2nd Army, at his headquarters in Alekszejevka on the Don River in October 1942. (War Correspondent Company

CONCLUSION

After World War I, due to peace treaty restrictions, Hungary was isolated politically, economically and militarily. However, cooperation between Italy and Hungary was active as early as the early 1920s and deepened with Mussolini's seizure of power, continuing until the end of his regime. Both sides benefited from this cooperation; Hungary obtained much-needed military armament and Italy was able to support its military industry by selling its military products and surplus materials captured during World War I.

Military-technical cooperation also played a significant, bidirectional and mutually beneficial role. Regular cooperation and board meetings ceased precisely in 1943, with the fall of the Mussolini government.

Italy played a significant role in rearming the Royal Hungarian Army and Air Force before World War II. At first, surplus Austro-Hungarian war materials were sold and smuggled into Hungary. Later, Italian assistance focused on three main areas: mechanization, armaments (mainly ammunition and artillery), and personal equipment.

Italian government loans made possible the practical execution of the Italian military program designed for Hungary.

Mechanization involved the delivery of vehicles and the sale of the Pavesi tractor license. The purchase of CV33/35 tanks helped the Hungarians create their own armored/mobile forces. From the mid-1930s to 1942, the backbone of the Royal Hungarian Air Force was Italian aircraft and pilots trained in Italy (not included in this book). Cooperation in artillery provided both countries with knowledge of each other's developments and weapons for sale, as well as artillery ammunition and the first modern heavy artillery pieces for the Hungarians. However, the reception of the Italian weapons was very mixed; by the time they were delivered, the Italian materials were either already obsolete or arrived with technical deficiencies and defects. Despite these drawbacks, Italian armaments largely constituted the rearmament of the Royal Hungarian Army in the first phase of World War II.

▲ Mixed-vehicle column led by a Fiat 508C hardtop passenger car painted in tricolor camouflage during the reconquest of Transylvanian territories in 1940. (Author collection)

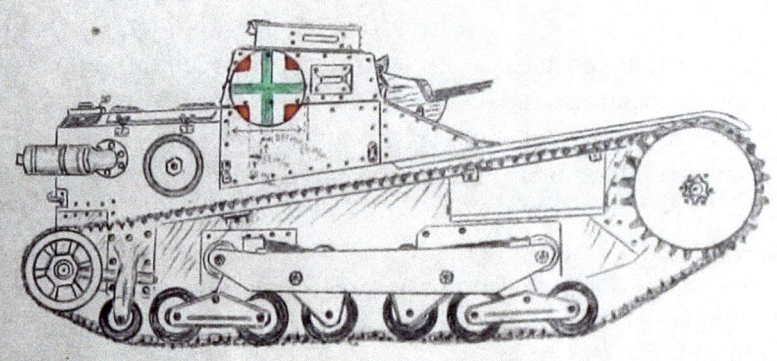
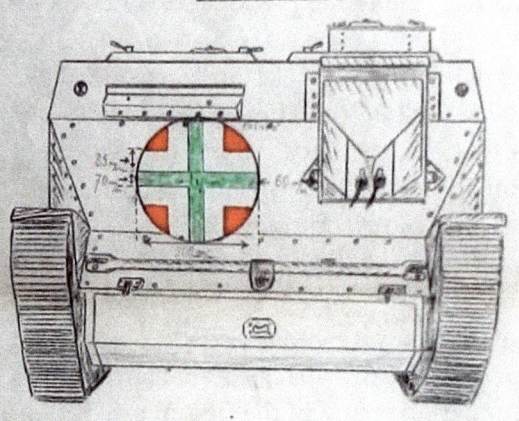
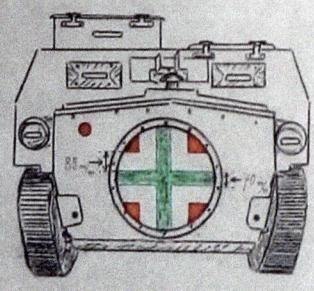
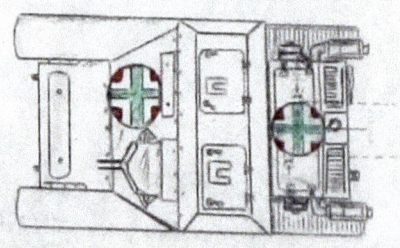

▲ Very interesting document showing the scheme of Hungarian insignia to be applied on Ansaldo light tanks in 1940. (Military Archive)

BIBLIOGRAPHY

HUNGARIAN BOOKS

Dr. Barczy Zoltán – Sárhidai Gyula : A Boforstól a Doráig, A magyar légvédelmi tüzérség 1914 – 1945, Petit Real 2008

Bíró Ádám – Éder Miklós – Sárhidai Gyula: A magyar királyi honvédség külföldi gyártású páncélos harcjárművei 1920- 1945, Petit Real, 2006

Bíró Ádám – Éder Miklós – Sárhidai Gyula: A magyar királyi honvédség hazai gyártású páncélos harcjárművei 1920- 1945, Petit Real, 2012

Bonhardt Attila – Sárhidai Gyula – Winkler László: A magyar királyi honvédség fegyverzete 1919-45 part 1, Zrínyi Kiadó 1992

Bonhardt Attila, Pánczél Mátyás, Végh Ferenc, Szerekes József, Hattyár István, Sári Szabolcs: A magyar páncélosalakulatok története, Zrínyi Kiadó 2015

Dombrády Loránd: A magyar gazdaság és a hadfelszerelés, 1938/44, Akadémia Kiadó 1981

..És újfent hadiidők! 1939-1945, Petit Real Könyvkiadó, 2005

Hajdú Ferenc – Sárhidai Gyula: A magyar királyi honvéd Haditechnikai Intézettől a HM Technológiai Hivatalig, HM Technológiai Hivatal 2005

Kis Gábor Ferenc: „Lovon, gyalog, autón, biciklin, vasúton.." A magyar királyi honvédség gyorscsapatai, Belvedere 2014

Dr. Varga A. József: Magyar autógyárak katonai járművei, 2008 Maróti

Dr. Varga A. József: A magyar katonai harc- és gépjármű fejlesztések története, HM kiadvány

ARTICLES

Hadtörténelmi Közlemények

Dombrándy Loránd: A horthysta katonai vezetés erőfeszítései a páncélos fegyvernem megteremtésére, HK 1969/2, 1970/4

Tóth Lajos: A Gyorshadtest a Szovjetunióban, HK 1966/2

Haditechnika

Bíró Ádám: A magyar páncélos fegyvernem kezdetei, az LK-II és FIAT-3000B harckocsik, 1993/2

Bíró Ádám: A magyar páncélos fegyvernem kezdetei, 2. rész, a FIAT Ansaldo 35M, 1993/3

Bíró Ádám: Az első magyar tervezésű harckocsi a V-4, 1992/4

Dr. Klemensits Péter: A magyar páncélos alakulatok a kárpátaljai hadműveletekben 1., 2014/5

Dr. Klemensits Péter: A magyar páncélos alakulatok a délvidéki hadműveletekben, 2014/6

Dr. Klemensits Péter: A Magyar páncélos erők a Szovjetunió elleni hadműveletekben – a Toldi könnyű harckocsi I. rész, 2016/1

Dr. Mujzer Péter: A magyar páncélos fegyvernem kezdetei I. rész, 2016/1

Dr. Mujzer Péter: A magyar páncélos fegyvernem szervezeti és fegyverzeti fejlesztése 1938-1942 I. rész, 2016/2

Dr. Mujzer Péter:A Magyar Királyi Honvédség páncélos szervezeteinek részvétele a Szovjetunió elleni hadműveletekben 1941-ben, 2017/3

Katona Újság

Söregi Zoltán: Adalékok a galántai csendőr karhatalmi zászlóalj történetéhez, 2011/1.

Militaria Modell

Éder Miklós: Magyar páncélos járművek alakulat jelzései, 1. rész, 1991 / 1

Éder Miklós: Magyar páncélos járművek alakulat jelzései, 2. rész, 1991/2

Éder Miklós: LK-II harckocsi a Magyar Honvédségnél, 1992/2

Éder Miklós: Magyar páncélos csapatok bőrruházata, 1992/4

Foreing Publications

Csaba Becze: Magyar steel, Mashroom Publication 2006

Dénes Bernád, Charles K. Kliment: Magyar Warriors, The history of the Royal Hungarian Armed Forces 1919-1945, volumen 1, Helion Publication, 2015

Dénes Bernád, Charles K. Kliment: Magyar Warriors, The history of the Royal Hungarian Armed Forces 1919-1945, volumen 2, Helion Publication, 2017

Patrick Cloutier: Three Kings: Axis Royal Armies on the Russian Front 1941, 2014

Petra Hamerli: Hungarian–Italian Economic Relations, 1927–1934, ELTE 2014

Victor Madej: South-Eastern Europe Axis Armies Handbook, Game Marketing Company, 1982

Military Intelligence Division: Order of Battle and Handbook of the Hungarian Armed Forces, 1944 US War Dep. (restricted)

Eduardo Gil Martinez: Fuerzas Acorazadas Húngaras 1939-43, Almena 2017

Péter Mujzer: Hungarian Mobile Forces 1920-45, Bayside Books, 2000

Péter Mujzer: Huns on Wheels, Hungarian Mobile Forces in WWII, Armoured, Cavalry, Bicycle Troops, Motorised Rifle, Mujzer and Partners Ltd., 2015

Péter Mujzer: Hungarian Armoured Forces in WWII, KAGERO Books, PHOTOSNIPER 26., 2017

Leo Niehorster: The Royal Hungarian Army 1920-45, Bayside Books, 1998

Nigel Thomas- László Pál Szabó: The Royal Hungarian Army in World War II, Ospery, 2008

Rex Trye: Mussolini's Soldiers, Motorbooks International, 1995

Anthony Tucker-Jones: Armored warfare and Hitler's allies 1941-1945, Pen&Sword, 2013

Steven Zaloga: Armored trains, Osprey, 2008

Steven Zaloga- James Grandsen: The Eastern Front, Arms and Armour, 1983

Steven Zaloga: Tanks of Hitler's eastern allies 1941-45, Osprey, 2013

TITOLI GIÀ PUBBLICATI - TITLES ALREADY PUBLISHING

www.ingramcontent.com/pod-product-compliance
Lightning Source LLC
LaVergne TN
LVHW081451060526
838201LV00050BA/1766